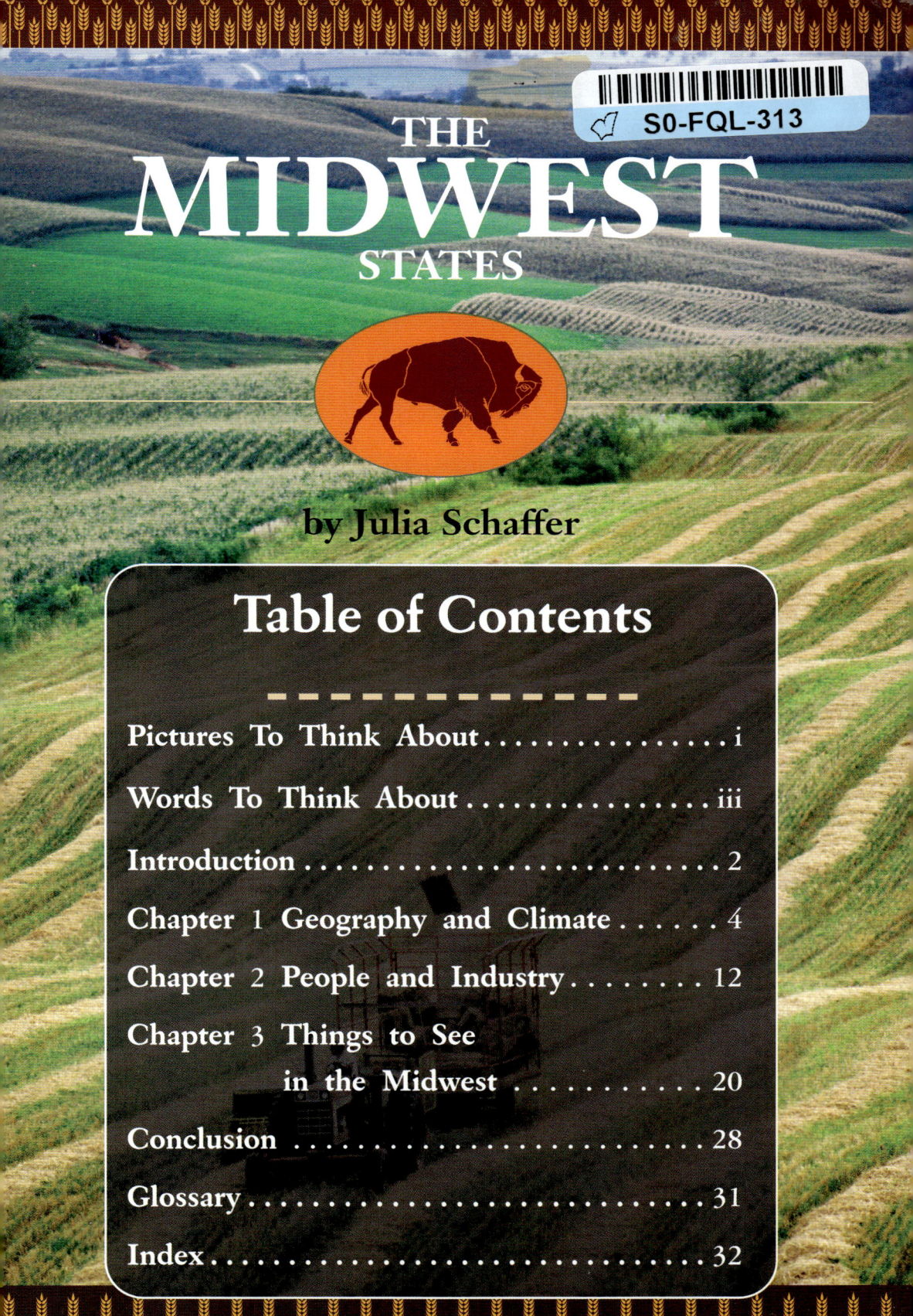

THE MIDWEST STATES

by Julia Schaffer

Table of Contents

Pictures To Think About i

Words To Think About iii

Introduction 2

Chapter 1 Geography and Climate 4

Chapter 2 People and Industry 12

Chapter 3 Things to See
in the Midwest 20

Conclusion 28

Glossary 31

Index 32

Pictures To Think About

The Midwest States

Words To Think About

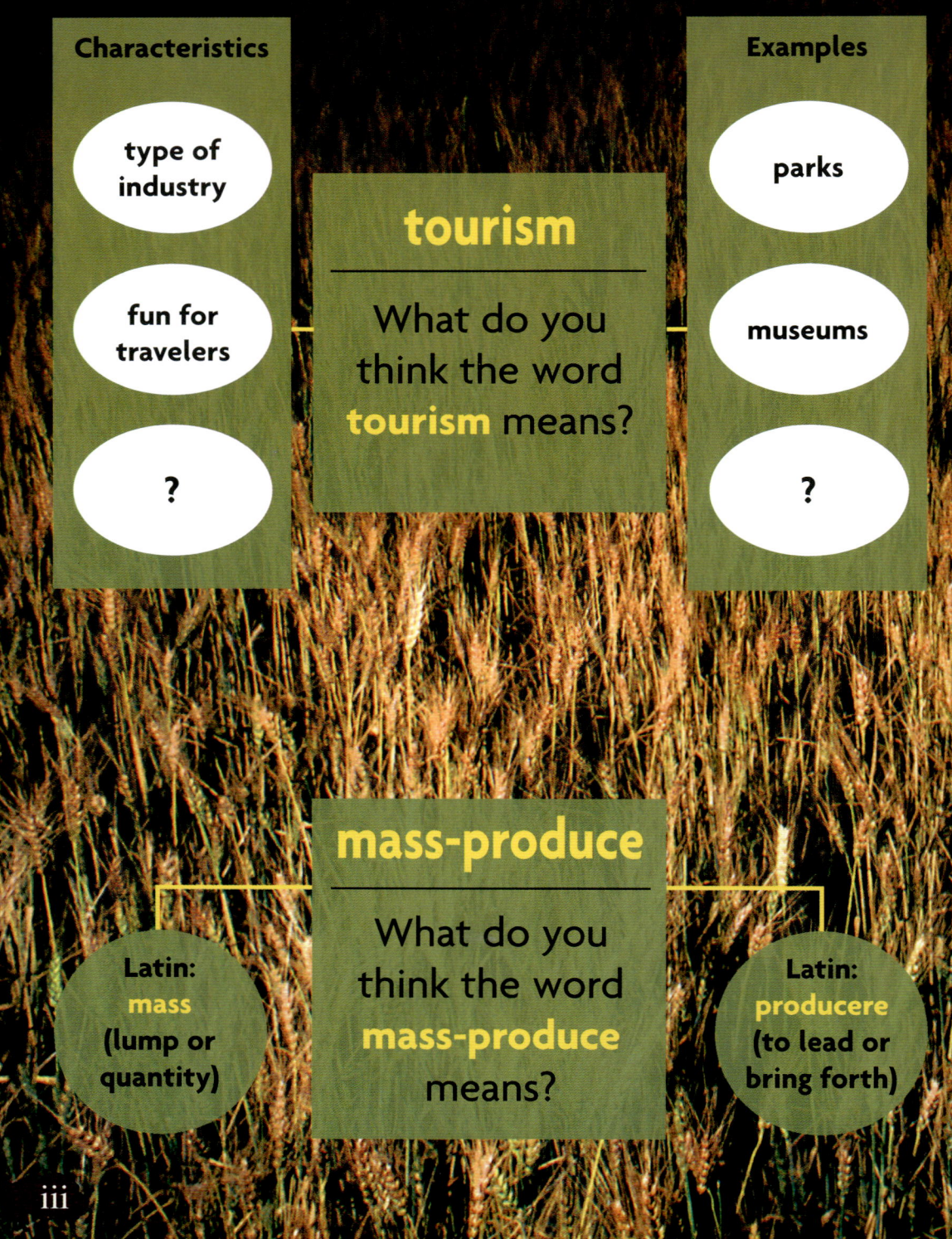

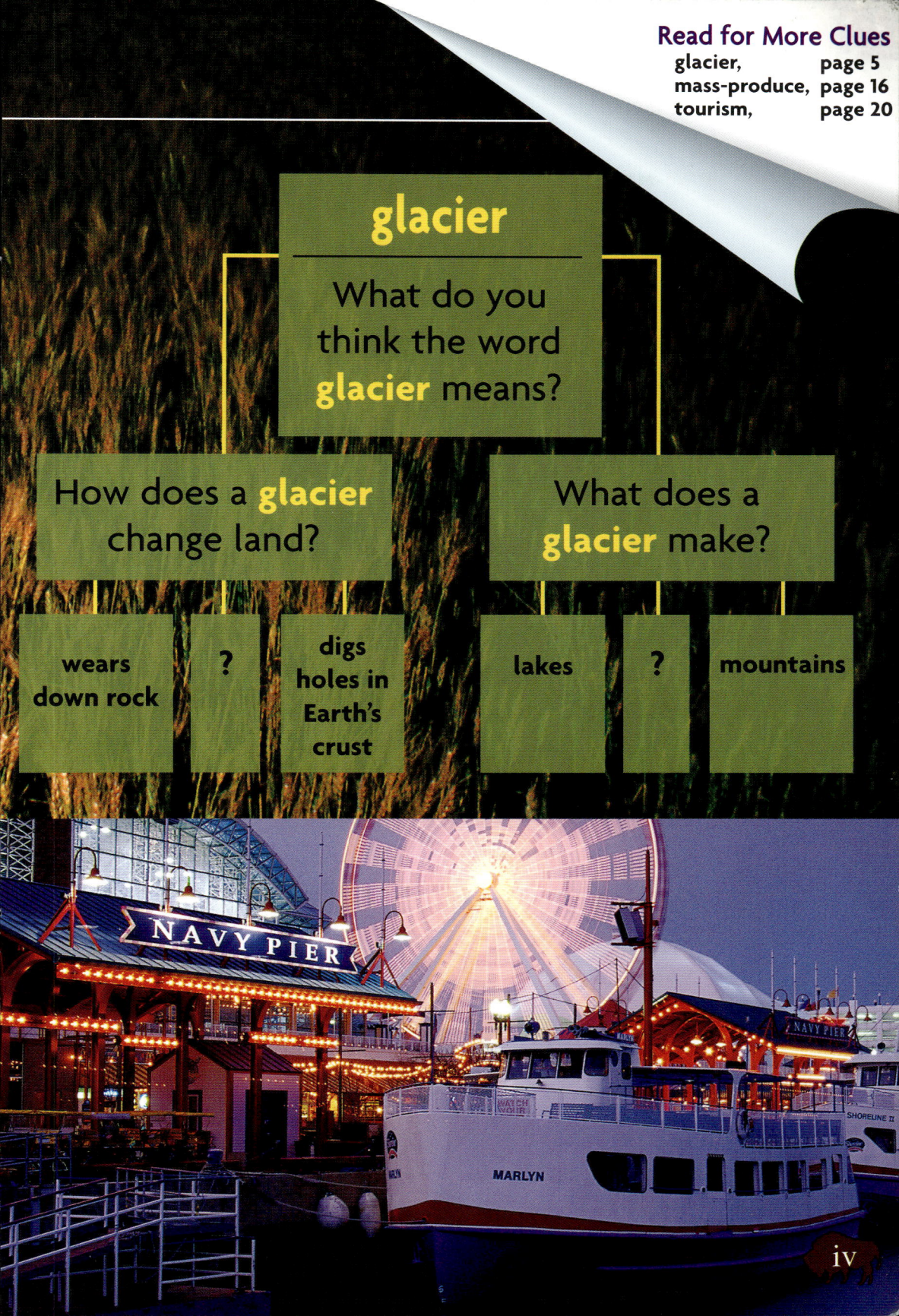

Read for More Clues
glacier, page 5
mass-produce, page 16
tourism, page 20

glacier

What do you think the word **glacier** means?

How does a **glacier** change land?

What does a **glacier** make?

wears down rock | ? | digs holes in Earth's crust

lakes | ? | mountains

iv

Introduction

Welcome to the Midwest. The Midwest is a **region** (REE-juhn) in the United States. A region is a large area. The states in a region share features. States in a region may have the same landforms. The people in a region share history. They may also share a way of life.

▼ Chicago, Illinois, the Midwest's biggest city, is a transportation center, or hub.

Midwest is short for "Middle West." In the early 1800s, the Midwest was the **frontier** (fruhn-TEER). The frontier was the edge of the country. Today, the Midwest is in the center of the country.

In this book, you will learn about the Midwest. You will visit two areas within the Midwest. You will visit the Great Lakes. You will also visit the flat, rolling lands of the Great **Plains** (PLAYNZ).

Read on. Discover the Midwest. Travel to "the crossroads of America."

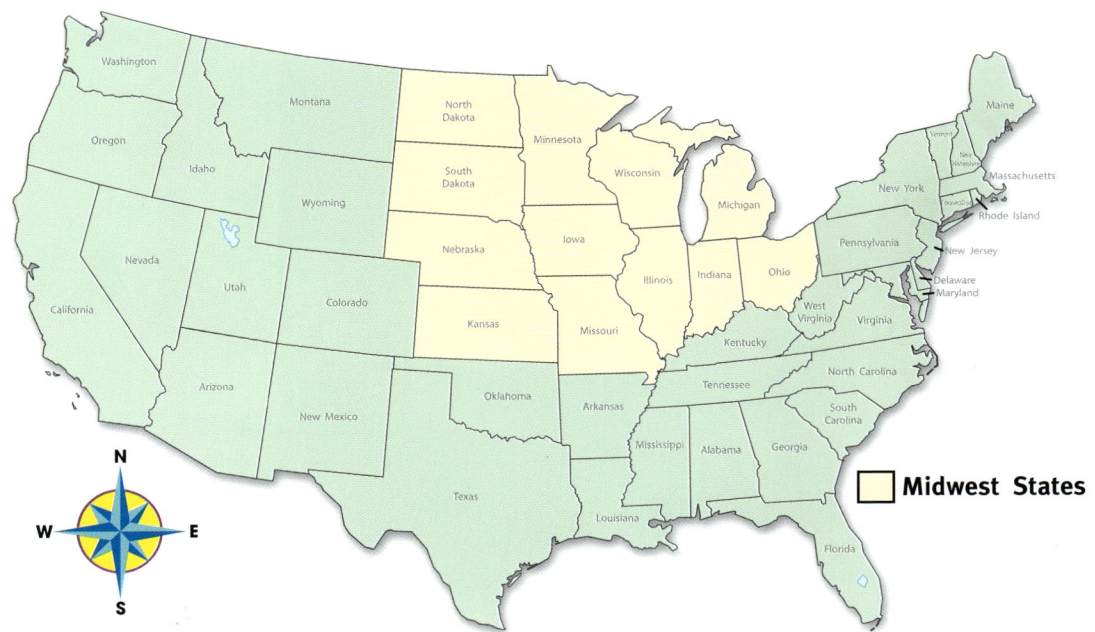

▲ Can you tell which state is in the exact center of this map? If you chose Kansas, you're right!

Chapter 1

Geography and Climate

This chapter is about the land of the Midwest. This chapter is also about the climate. You will visit the Great Lakes and Great Plains. You will find out how these regions are alike and different. You will also learn about the weather. Hang on to your hat!

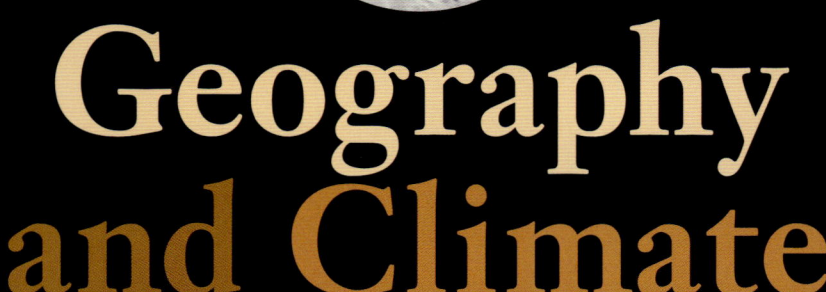

▲ The states in the Great Lakes region are Ohio, Indiana, Illinois, Michigan, Wisconsin, and Minnesota.

▲ A camera in space took this photo of the Great Lakes.

The Great Lakes Region

The Great Lakes states share many features. They have rivers, forests, rolling hills, and rich soil. Many forests are found in the north. Much of the farmland is in the south.

The region also has five very large lakes. The lakes are called the Great Lakes. The Great Lakes are huge. They can be seen from the moon. The lakes are the largest source of fresh water in the United States.

If you spread all the water in the Great Lakes across the forty-eight connected states, there would be 9.5 feet (2.9 meters) of water covering every inch. Even the world's tallest basketball players would have two feet (.6 meters) of water over their heads.

What made these giant lakes? Long ago, a **glacier** (GLAY-shuhr) covered this region. A glacier is a giant mass of ice. As it melted, the glacier dug deep holes. The ice melted. Then the deep holes filled with water. The holes became the Great Lakes.

▲ On a hot summer day, people swim in Lake Michigan, one of the five Great Lakes.

CHAPTER 1

Rivers, Islands, and Dunes

Michigan has many rivers, lakes, and streams. Stand anywhere in the state. You will be no more than 6 miles (9.6 kilometers) from a waterway!

These waterways have hundreds of tiny islands. Many of them have sand **dunes** (DOONZ). Dunes are hills made of sand. Dunes are shaped by wind.

Long ago, people used the waterways to travel. Today, people use the waterways for boating, fishing, and swimming.

▲ rivers of the Midwest

GEOGRAPHY AND CLIMATE

Piles of Snow

The Great Lakes have a big effect on the weather. The air over the lakes is always moist, or wet. The moist air keeps the area from getting very hot or very cold. In winter, the moisture turns into snow. It snows a lot in this region. One year, Lake Superior got 350 inches (889 centimeters) of snow.

It's a Fact

The heaviest snows in the Great Lakes region are caused by the "lake effect." When very cold air blows over the warm water of the lakes, big clouds form. When the clouds reach land, they dump piles of snow on the shore.

▲ People in Bayfield, Wisconsin, ice fish on Lake Superior. The tree marks an "ice road" across the lake.

 **Point**

Talk About It
What problems might a community face with 350 inches (889 centimeters) of snow in one year? How could people plan ahead for a situation like this? What special equipment might they need?

CHAPTER 1

The Great Plains Region

The Great Plains is another region in the Midwest. Plains are flat, rolling lands. The plains have rich soil and are covered with grasses. The plains have few trees. The plains are great for farming. People grow wheat, corn, soybeans, and other crops there.

Look at the map on the next page. You can see the Great Plains states. A big river runs through the plains. It is called the Missouri River. People use rivers and streams to transport things. People also use these waterways for **irrigation** (eer-ih-GAY-shuhn). Irrigation is a way of bringing water to dry land.

Careers
Boat Captain

Boat captains spend their days on the water. They pilot fishing boats, passenger boats, and boats carrying supplies. The captain decides the speed and direction of the boat. He makes sure everyone on board stays safe. To be a captain, you need to know math and geography.

▲ The Missouri River is the longest river in the United States. It feeds into the Mississippi River, the second-longest river.

GEOGRAPHY AND CLIMATE

Extreme Temperatures

In the winter, blizzards sweep across the plains. In the summer, a hot sun shines. Big storms like tornadoes can start up suddenly. In Nebraska, people have a saying: "If you don't like the weather, wait five minutes."

▲ Be prepared! On the Great Plains, the weather changes fast.

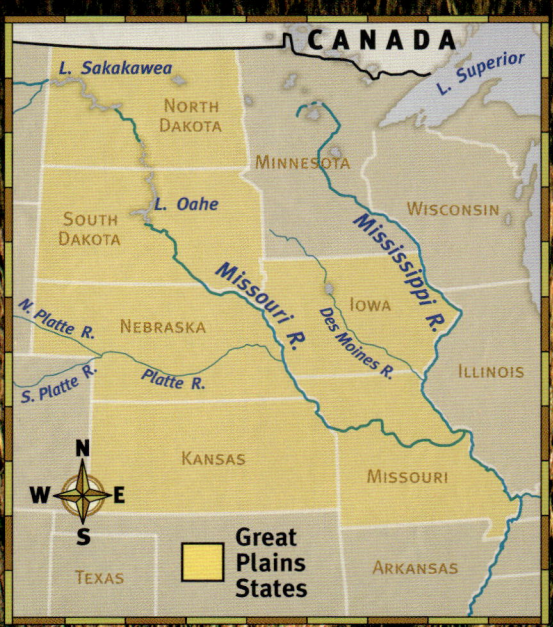

9

CHAPTER 1

Droughts

Sometimes rain does not fall. A long time without rain is called a **drought** (DROWT). Droughts happen on the plains. Sometimes, droughts cause dust storms. In the 1930s, Kansas was called the Dust Bowl. The dust storms were so thick that they blocked the sun. Whole farms were destroyed. Farmers called the storms "black blizzards."

▲ In 1934, one storm blew piles of dust as far north as Illinois.

Primary Source

In his novel *The Grapes of Wrath*, John Steinbeck describes the start of a dust storm: "Little by little the sky was darkened by the mixing dust, and the wind felt over the earth, loosened the dust and carried it away."

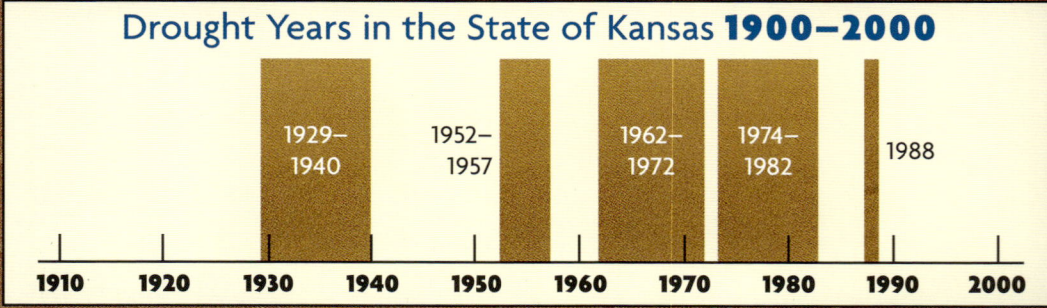

▲ In the United States, droughts occur roughly every twenty-five years.

GEOGRAPHY AND CLIMATE

Droughts also affect South Dakota. Strong winds blow dry soil across the land. Farmers must keep the soil moist. This stops storms from hurting crops. People in the Midwest have to use water wisely.

Water Underground

A body of water below the earth helps farmers in Kansas, Nebraska, and South Dakota irrigate their land. The Ogallala (oh-guh-LAH-lah) Aquifer is 400 feet (121.9 meters) deep. It lies under eight different states. Farmers first pumped its water in 1911. The aquifer dates back to the Ice Age.

▲ The use of water from the Ogallala Aquifer helps keep farms healthy and green.

Chapter 2

People and Industry

In 1800, the United States was smaller. The country ended at the Mississippi River. The Great Lakes were part of the country. The Great Plains were not. Then, in 1803, President Thomas Jefferson bought more land. France sold the Louisiana Territory for $15 million. It was a huge piece of land. It stretched from the Mississippi River to the Rocky Mountains. The territory became fifteen states. Six of those states are today part of the Midwest.

◀ **The Louisiana Purchase doubled the size of the United States.**

Two mapmakers went out to explore the land. Their names were Meriwether Lewis and William Clark. The men traveled 2,500 miles (4,023.4 kilometers). They drew everything they saw. They made careful maps.

Historical Perspective

Lewis and Clark were mapmakers. They explored a new area. Then they drew a map of it by hand. Today, mapmakers draw maps on computers. They base their maps on photographs taken from the air.

▲ Lewis and Clark in Missouri with Sacajawea in 1805

▲ This map shows the routes taken by Lewis and Clark. It was copied from maps made by William Clark.

CHAPTER 2

Moving West

At first, few people moved to the new land. Then, in 1862, the government began to give free land to anyone who would farm it. Many people rushed to settle the new land. The land was good for farming.

▲ Ads like this one encouraged settlers to move west.

▲ railroad construction on the Great Plains, 1875

PEOPLE AND INDUSTRY

In 1869, the railroad was finished. Trains brought more people west. Farmers used trains to ship their goods to markets.

Railroads made life better. New roads, canals, and steamboats also made life better. New machines helped farmers grow more food. At first, farmers just grew food for their families. Machines helped them grow enough food to sell to others.

Eyewitness Account

Mary Elizabeth Munkers was ten years old in 1846. That year, her family traveled across the Great Plains. "I remember when we were camped..., the whole sky became black as ink. A terrific wind came up, which blew the covers off the wagons and blew down the tents... The rain came down in bucketfuls, drenching us to the skin. There wasn't a tent in the camp that held against the terrific wind."

CHAPTER 2

Industry in the Midwest

Farmers grew food. Workers made food products. The food **industry** (IHN-duhs-tree) began to grow in the Midwest. Industries are groups of businesses. The businesses in an industry make the same types of products.

The machine industry also grew. Factories made machines of all kinds. In the early 1900s, the Midwest began to **mass-produce** (MASS pruh-DOOS) cars. That means to make many cars quickly. Today, making cars is still a big business in the Midwest.

They Made A Difference

Henry Ford made a car that many people could afford. The car was the Model T. Ford also thought of a new way to make cars. He used an assembly line. Workers stood in one place while cars went by on a moving belt. Each worker added a part and then the car moved on down the line. Workers could mass-produce cars. They were able to make thousands of cars each day instead of just a few.

PEOPLE AND INDUSTRY

Farming, Logging, and Manufacturing in the Great Lakes

People in the Great Lakes region grow food for the whole country. Today, Wisconsin is the biggest maker of cheese in the nation. Michigan grows the most cherries. Wood from forests in Minnesota is used for building. Paper for books also comes from forests.

The Great Lakes region also has other resources. This area has iron, copper, and coal. We use these things to make cars, tools, and energy.

▲ Pennies are made of copper. Copper is mined in Wisconsin.

▲ Today, people work together to make sure there are enough forests as well as a strong lumber industry in the region.

17

CHAPTER 2

A Breadbasket

Do you eat bread, pasta, or cereal? Chances are the grain in those foods was grown in the Midwest. Kansas grows more wheat than any other state. The Great Plains are called the nation's breadbasket.

Q & A with Paul Bischke, farmer

Q: Where is your farm?
A: I have 200 acres in North Dakota. As farms go, that's pretty small.
Q: What do you grow?
A: Grains—alfalfa, rye, and winter wheat.
Q: How much winter wheat do you produce?
A: Last year I had about 3,000 tons.
Q: I thought you said your farm was small!
A: Trust me, that's small.
Q: What's the best thing about farming?
A: Watching things grow. Making them grow. Doing work that is valuable.

▲ In one year, farmers in Kansas can grow enough wheat to make six loaves of bread for every person on Earth.

PEOPLE AND INDUSTRY

Food Processing and Mining

Missouri has 100,000 farms. Farmers grow wheat and corn. They also raise animals for meat and milk. Then they make these products into the food you buy in stores. This is called food processing. It is one of the most important industries in the Midwest.

▲ Nebraska processes more beef than any other state.

Mining is also an important industry. North and South Dakota have oil, natural gas, and gold.

Transportation Hub

The Midwest is in the middle of the country. Many people pass through the region. People pass through on trains, buses, and cars. They pass through in trucks, boats, and airplanes, too. One part of Indiana is a busy hub. It is one of the most traveled places in the nation.

Primary Source

Do you recognize the song lyrics below? What part of the country do you think is being described?

"O beautiful for spacious skies / For amber waves of grain / For purple mountain majesties / Above the fruited plain!"

This song is describing the Midwest!

Chapter 3

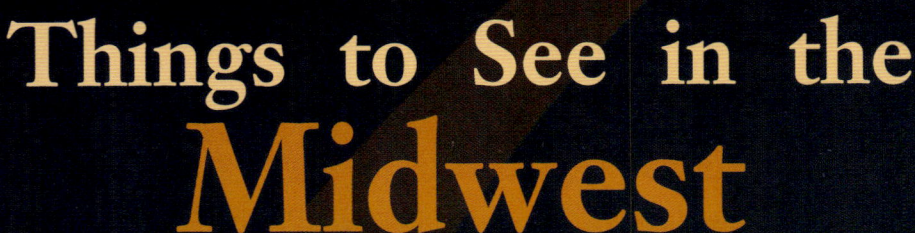

Things to See in the Midwest

Another important industry is **tourism** (TOR-ih-zuhm). The Midwest has many fun things to see and do. Many people go to Chicago, Illinois. This is the biggest city in the region.

◀ The world's first Ferris wheel opened in Chicago in 1893.

▲ Bob Dylan

It's a Fact

Have you heard of Chuck Berry and Bob Dylan? These musicians are both from the Midwest. Visit the Rock and Roll Hall of Fame in Cleveland, Ohio, to learn more about these and other musicians.

Big Cities

Chicago is on Lake Michigan. The city is sometimes called "the third coast." You can see great art. You can eat a tasty sausage. Or you can ride the first Ferris wheel.

St. Louis is another great city. St. Louis is in Missouri. In the 1800s, many people left St. Louis to go west. That is why it is called the "Gateway to the West." You can see a giant silver arch there. You can also take a ride on the mighty Mississippi River. It is a great way to see the city.

You can ride a tram to ▶ the top of the Gateway Arch for a great view of St. Louis.

CHAPTER 3

Historic Sites

Many tourists like history. Kansas and Nebraska have historic trails. You can still walk the trails today. You can see landmarks. One landmark is Chimney Rock. Landmarks like this helped guide the early settlers.

How did the early settlers send mail? Back then, they sent mail on horseback. The Pony Express was their mail service. Riders delivered letters all the way to California!

Historical Perspective

In 1860, the Pony Express could deliver a letter from Missouri to California in ten days. Today, a letter sent express travels the same distance in one day. With e-mail, faxes, and phones, you can send a message in seconds.

▼ a pony express rider on his route

THINGS TO SEE IN THE MIDWEST

In the mid-1800s, many slaves fled to Ohio. The slaves were looking for freedom in the North. They went to the homes of people who protected slaves. These places were known as stations along the Underground Railroad. In Ohio, you can still visit these historic homes.

◀ With its pointy shape, Nebraska's Chimney Rock stood out as a signpost to the settlers going west.

▲ This house in Ohio belonged to John Rankin. Rankin was one of the organizers of the Underground Railroad.

CHAPTER 3

Midwest People and Land

Would you like to travel across the Midwest? You will see and do many things. Spend the day at a dairy farm in Wisconsin. Feed a calf milk from a bottle. Gather eggs from a henhouse. Then sit down to eat a farm-fresh meal.

▲ Visitors to a Wisconsin dairy farm help out with daily chores.

▲ These unusual rock shapes helped give the Badlands its name. Most visitors today think the park is anything but bad.

✓ Point

Visualize
Imagine yourself as a dairy farmer. How would you spend your day? What chores would you do? What would you do for fun? What would you be sure to show visitors?

THINGS TO SEE IN THE MIDWEST

Next, go to South Dakota. Visit a place shaped by nature. In Badlands National Park, you can see how wind and water changed the land. Go after a rainstorm. You will see bright red bands on the rocks.

Then go to Michigan. Sleeping Bear Dunes is a great place to visit. This place has 35 miles (56.3 kilometers) of beach, forests, rocks, and, of course, dunes.

▲ On a hike through Badlands National Park, you might see a buffalo.

CHAPTER 3

Special Events

You will always find fun events in the Midwest. Do you like fast cars? Each May, Indiana has a big car race. The race is 500 miles (804.7 kilometers) long. The race is called the Indy 500.

▼ The Indianapolis (in-dee-uh-NA-puh-lis) 500 is the biggest one-day sporting event in the world.

Primary Source

Here's a song about Iowa from the musical *State Fair*:

"Our state fair is a great state fair / Don't miss it, don't even be late. / It's dollars to doughnuts that our state fair / Is the best state fair in our state!"

▲ If you visit the Iowa State Fair, you can see a statue carved entirely out of butter.

THINGS TO SEE IN THE MIDWEST

Every August, crowds visit the Iowa State Fair. People go to see pigs, goats, vegetables, and flowers. You can also see tractors and farm equipment. One of the highlights is the Butter Cow. It is a life-size cow made from 600 pounds (272.2 kilograms) of butter!

In North Dakota, you can go to a **powwow** (POW-wow). Every September, Native American tribes come together. The powwow is how the tribes celebrate life. People at the powwow sing and dance. It is a time for family and friends to enjoy each other. Visitors are welcome.

The United Tribes ▶ International Powwow is one of the biggest powwows in North America.

Conclusion

The Midwest is a special place. It has a rich history and landscape. It has rivers, forests, dunes, and plains. It has grasslands and lakes, too.

Settlers first moved to the Midwest to farm. Then people opened factories. Today, the region is still the center of farming. It also has many other industries.

It's a Fact
Mount Rushmore is a giant monument to America. The monument is carved into a mountain in South Dakota. Do you recognize these faces? One was the first president of the United States (George Washington). Another was the president who purchased the Louisiana Territory (Thomas Jefferson). Another one became a conservationist (Theodore Roosevelt). Another was born in Illinois (Abraham Lincoln).

The Midwest has busy cities. It has pretty rural landscapes. You can go to state fairs, powwows, and car races.

Would you like to do those things and more? Then visit the Midwest!

Paul Bunyan is a fictional folk hero. According to legend, he was a Minnesota logger. It was said that he could clear whole forests with one swing of his axe.

CONCLUSION

Getting to the Midwest is easy. The region is the transportation hub of the United States. Wherever you go in the nation, you will probably go through the Midwest.

Glossary

drought   (DROWT) a period of time with a severe lack of rain or other moisture (page 10)

dune   (DOON) a hill made of sand and shaped by wind (page 6)

frontier   (fruhn-TEER) the far edge of a country where people are just beginning to settle (page 3)

glacier   (GLAY-shuhr) a large, slowly moving chunk of ice (page 5)

industry   (IHN-duhs-tree) a group of businesses that produce and sell similar products or services (page 16)

irrigation   (eer-ih-GAY-shuhn) a way of bringing water to dry land (page 8)

mass-produce   (MASS pruh-DOOS) to make lots of the same thing, usually by machine (page 16)

plains   (PLAYNZ) large, flat regions covered with grass but with few trees (page 3)

powwow   (POW-wow) a Native American ceremony (page 27)

region   (REE-juhn) a large area made up of places that share some features, such as geography and climate (page 2)

tourism   (TOR-ih-zuhm) an industry that provides goods and services to people who travel for pleasure (page 20)

Index

Badlands, 24–25
Chicago, 20–21
drought, 10–11
dune, 6, 25, 28
Ford, Henry, 16
frontier, 3
glacier, 5
Great Lakes, 3–5, 7, 12, 17
Indianapolis 500, 26
industry, 16–17, 19–20, 28
Iowa State Fair, 26–27
irrigation, 8
Jefferson, Thomas, 12, 28
Lake Michigan, 21
Lake Superior, 7
Lewis and Clark, 13
Louisiana Territory, 12, 28
mass-produce, 16
Mississippi River, 8, 12, 21
Missouri River, 8
plains, 3–4, 8–10, 12, 14–15, 18, 28
Pony Express, 22
powwow, 27, 29
railroad, 14–15
region, 2, 4–5, 7–8, 17, 19–20, 28, 30
St. Louis, 21
tourism, 20
Underground Railroad, 23